MW00668206

"…benefits every employee by providing fresh insights into their job, their organization, and the mutually beneficial relationship between the two."

Angelo Lynn
Publisher
Addison Independent newspaper

A partial list of discerning readers who purchased the first edition of *Water Cooler Wisdom...*

- University of Phoenix
- City of San Diego
- Department of Defense
- Bibb County Board of Education
- University of Chicago
- Indianapolis Power & Light Co.
- General Pump U.S. Inc.
- Toro Corporation
- Hager Hinge Co.
- Smugglers' Notch Resort
- Cutler-Hammer
- Ameritas Life Insurance
- Omaha Steaks International
- Allstate Insurance Co.
- New Hampshire Grocers Association
- Northwestern Mutual Life
- NYNEX
- State Farm Insurance Co.
- Valley Regional Hospital
- Rochester Gas & Electric
- Sara Lee Refrigerated Foods
- Cincinnati Gas & Electric
- Federated Department Stores
- Martin Franchises Inc.

- Ohio Industrial Training Program
- One-Hour Martinizing
- General Electric Company
- Houston Compressed Steel
- Augusta Hospital Corporation
- BFG Industries, Inc.
- Goodyear Tire & Rubber Co.
- Shady Brook Farms
- U.S. Postal Service
- A.N. Derringer
- American Heart Association
- American Red Cross
- Olsten Staffing Services
- Edlund Company
- Green Mountain Power
- Hemmings Motor News
- John McKenzie Packing
- Penn Financial Services
- Porter Medical Center
- Spaulding High School
- State of Vermont Environmental Board
- University of Vermont
- Food Services of America
- Allied Signal

See page 189 to order additional copies and for information on how to contact us.

Water Cooler
Wisdom

50 Quick Tips For Workplace Success!

Published by ClientKeep Inc., P.O. Box 665, Shelburne, VT 05482-0665

Portions of this book previously appeared in:
How to Mean Business - A Pocket Guide To More Success At Work
by Scott Delman

Library of Congress Control Number: 2002090713
Delman, Scott
Water Cooler Wisdom – 50 Quick Tips For Workplace Success
by Scott Delman
ISBN: 0-9645063-1-9

Orders and Inquiries: www.WaterCoolerWisdom.biz (800) 974-5337
Fax: (802) 985-5656

Edited by Andrew Yavelow, Hinesburg, VT
Designed by IdeaDesignGroup.com, Colchester, VT
Printed in USA by L. Brown & Sons Printing, Inc., Barre, VT

*For Vivian and all the other hardworking
people I know who labor to make their
company or organization more successful
and a more fulfilling place to work.*

Introduction

About a decade ago, I worked with Vivian, a down-to-earth woman in her forties with a high school equivalency education. We worked for a company with all of the customary departments: sales, service, customer service, parts, accounting, advertising, administration, and so on. Vivian worked in the parts area as a "gopher" – straightening, cleaning and assisting everyone else.

Vivian's regular duties included cleaning the warehouse floor. She did an average job at best and often appeared discouraged, finding no pride or pleasure in her work.

Seeing her struggle was disheartening. I felt compelled to help her understand how significant her work was to our company. As we conversed, I asked why she thought cleaning the warehouse floors was important. She responded, "I don't know, I guess it's so dirt doesn't build up so they're easier to clean." What followed was the beginning of a change in Vivian's work life and, in part, my inspiration for writing *Water Cooler Wisdom*.

As we talked, she realized that clean floors meant even more: they provide a margin of safety that helps prevent injury; they symbolize a department whose members work with pride and operate with professional standards; they impress our customers, distinguish us from the competition, and enhance our reputation. Not only that, her department was also setting an example that others in the company might follow.

Vivian understood. A lightbulb went on. Her posture changed; she sat taller and smiled. She realized that keeping the floors clean was an essential job that had important ramifications. She recognized that she was responsible for more than a lack of dirt. She realized that by doing a professional job, *she* would make a difference in the company overall.

From that day forward, the floors were cleaner than ever. Other people took notice and commented on the improvement in both her attitude and her work. Vivian began to take pride in what she did. She believed more in herself and her importance in the company. The bottom line is that Vivian became happier and more successful.

I spoke to Vivian just the other day. It has been more than ten years since we worked together and I wanted to check the accuracy of my recollection. She answered her phone with a cheery voice. We recounted our experience together and she brought me up to date on her career. She said, "Scott, I remember those earlier days – a lot has happened since then. Now I have one of the most important jobs in the company. I am the inventory control shipping and receiving specialist. I place orders, coordinate and locate parts, and make sure everyone has what they need. They even offered me a supervisory position. I am planning to retire from here."

Vivian's story is true and illustrates what I have been noticing for years – when people understand why and how they are important and how they make their organization better, their self-esteem rises, their sense of pride grows, and they do more and better work. They become "turned on" and approach their work with a more open-minded attitude – they are more willing to learn. They contribute not only their skill, but also their knowledge. And their organization becomes better overall.

Water Cooler Wisdom is a catalyst – a tool to jump-start the process of knowing and using professional standards, learning how to best approach your work, and understanding the "what's in it" for you and for your organization. Much like the conversation I had with Vivian, this book will help stimulate a change in how you see your importance and value. You will discover that you are capable of being much more significant at work.

How you use *Water Cooler Wisdom* is up to both you and your organization. First and foremost, it is a book that you should read. Inside you will find fifty Quick-Tips. If you do nothing more than reflect on them, you will become enlightened and inspired to do better at work...not because the boss said so, but because you want to.

To benefit even more, use the workbooks at the end of each section. Here you will discover that you know a lot more about what is important in your place of business than you customarily think about each day. You will come up with ideas to improve your own work, your department, and your organization at large. You will more clearly see your own potential.

Using *Water Cooler Wisdom* to its highest potential becomes a joint effort when the management team joins in the game. Now is when they will look for your ideas and suggestions and collaborate in making changes. Your company will utilize more of your talent than ever before. Everyone benefits – people are happier, and the workplace culture reflects it!

There are a few things that I ask you to keep in mind as you read *Water Cooler Wisdom*.

★ If your boss gave you this copy of *Water Cooler Wisdom*, please thank her or him. Whatever your boss's motive, you will benefit by reading it.
★ If you are a boss (or manager), give a copy of this book to your employees, get involved and become a coach. Coaches help people become better at what they do by ensuring their success. Coaching is more valuable than telling.
★ This book is about you, not them. Be sure to participate in the process of self-inspection (where can you improve?) as well as organizational inspection (where can they improve?).

* If you understand strategic planning, you will easily recognize the limitless value of reviewing all of the filled-in workbooks from the organization. Important ideas and information abound. You have in your hand a tool to harvest them.
* Expect that your personal life will improve as your professional life does. The goals, values, and principles defined in each of the Quick-Tips in this book apply universally.
* Know that we all have customers – we all serve someone. Some are "external customers" – those we serve who are outside our organization. Others are "internal customers" – our co-workers. The service that we give to both these groups needs to be based on the same high standards.
* There is a difference between a customer and a client. See the definitions in Quick-Tips #13 and #14 but don't get hung-up on words. Use whichever label is more customary in your industry.
* This book applies to you, your department, company, organization, business, institution, not-for-profit, etc. These organizational labels are interchangeable in the text, and the concepts apply universally among them all.
* If you are a student or new to the workforce, use the Quick-Tips as a road map to professional performance. Starting your career on the right foot will serve you for years to come.
* Remember, *Water Cooler Wisdom* is about opportunity. Read it when you are ready to improve and you will. Your happiness and your success are in your own hands.

Scott Delman

Water Cooler Wisdom

50 Quick Tips For Workplace Success!

www.WaterCoolerWisdom.biz

Contents

Contents (*continued*)

Using the Workbooks in *Water Cooler Wisdom*

The big picture...

The workbooks in *Water Cooler Wisdom* are designed to help you think comprehensively about your workplace. Like an onion with its numerous layers, you have scads of knowledge and creative, untapped ideas that go far beyond your daily work routine. By using these workbooks honestly and thoughtfully, you will get the chance to utilize even more of your talent than you usually do.

Why use it?

For starters, you deserve it. All of us deserve a chance to express our opinion. Using the workbooks properly will provide the chance to formulate, clarify, and document your thoughts. The suggestions you make can help you be a happier, better worker and help your organization be a better place to work. Most organizations don't have the resources or time to seek out input from the workforce at large; that is a privilege usually reserved for a small core of management staff. By using these workbooks, you will be contributing important and often critical information. You will be involved in "strategic thinking," a process that mines suggestions and input from those who participate.

How is this information useful?

There are three levels of utilizing the information from the workbook exercises:

Level One: Read each section, fill out the workbook, and consider your own performance. By answering the questions thoughtfully and honestly, you will become aware of your opportunities to improve.

Level Two: Your management team collects the workbook from the staff and considers the suggestions before them. By doing so, they have extended their reach for strategic knowledge from the usual small group to the entire staff. The volume of information and input they receive will include essential information, suggestions, and perspectives to better manage their organization.

Level Three: Your managers team up with you and your co-workers. Here is where you work together and use your input to amplify your organization's strengths and to make improvements. You will be asked to contribute beyond your usual workload – to be creative and think in different ways. You may get your first chance to give your "all" and will soon realize how worthwhile you are to a team. Your organization will get tremendous value from having you as an employee as well as getting the information they need to be competitive and profitable. The results can be staggering.

How it works...

Read a section of *Water Cooler Wisdom*. Each of the seven sections contains from four to fourteen Quick-Tips. Each Quick-Tip takes about one minute to read. Reflect on each Quick-Tip as you read it. Think about your company or organization, your marketplace, your clients, your vendors, your co-workers, your manager and your own performance. Ask yourself how you, your company and others you work with should perform in this area. Note what is going really well. Also make note of where things can improve. Ask yourself what can be done to achieve better results. What should the company do? What should your manager do? What should your co-workers do? What should you do? After you have considered your thoughts from the section you just read, go to the workbook and follow the instructions carefully. Off-the-cuff answers might help a little but won't offer you or your organization the same benefit as more deeply thought out ideas. Be sure to apply your most considered suggestions.

Knowing Your Organization

The workplace is like a home, the workforce like a family. Everything that happens ultimately affects everyone else. Both employers and staff need to keep this basic tenet in mind: progress requires cooperation. Success is built on working together toward the ultimate good of your organization. Remember and use these six Quick-Tips to strengthen your personal effectiveness and worth within your workplace "family."

YOUR COMPANY
OR ORGANIZATION
... is a mutual dependency

#1 Your Company or Organization

definition

Your Company is the organization that pays you in exchange for your support. Each of you is dependent on the other.

what to do

See your company or organization as a community. Devote yourself to its ongoing health and growth by understanding your role and performing at your full potential. Treat every one of your co-workers with appreciation and respect. Behave proactively, supportively, and responsibly.

why to do it

Everything you do at work affects your company or organization. By performing your job with skill and a positive attitude, you create a more desirable work environment and help your company project a more successful image; your work life – and the work life of everyone around you – becomes more meaningful.

remember...

Only a successful organization can provide jobs for its workers.

THE
WORKPLACE

... is your work area

#2 The Workplace

definition

Your Workplace is the location, building, office area, machinery, equipment, and emotional environment in, with, and around which you work every day.

what to do

Contribute to the kind of workplace that you value. Treat every co-worker like a client, and every client like a friend – with honesty, sincerity, and respect. Do excellent work, and speak highly of your peers and your company. Cooperate, show you care, and be responsible for your own actions. Work within guidelines, be neat and clean, and always work safely.

why to do it

When every worker contributes to a good workplace, work quality is higher, and productivity and profits go up. Teamwork is stronger and your company becomes a more stable and enjoyable place to work.

remember...

*A good workplace is like a good home –
supportive, safe, and well worth investing in.*

YOUR
MANAGER

... needs your cooperation

QUICK-TIP

#3 Your Manager

definition

Your Manager is the person who provides and facilitates your job, and is responsible for everything you do in the workplace.

what to do

For the best results, team up with your manager. Contribute your best by approaching your work proactively, responding positively to training opportunities, and being punctual with assignments. Communicate, cooperate, and allow your manager to help you. And, when appropriate, express your appreciation.

why to do it

You and your manager depend on each other for success; your job is to do good work, and your manager's job is to help that happen. When you and your manager communicate effectively and work together, your work environment becomes more pleasant, more productive, and more rewarding. You, your manager, and your organization will all be more successful.

remember...

Cooperating with your manager helps you both become more valuable employees.

CO-WORKERS

… are your business partners

#4   Co-Workers

definition

Your Co-Workers are all the other people who work at your place of business. Each one of you has an impact on all the others.

what to do

Treat co-workers as your work family: with courtesy, respect, and support. Help them succeed at their jobs, and give co-workers the same high level of commitment, work, and service that you give your clients.

why to do it

The quality of your work life and the success of your business or organization are entirely up to you and your co-workers. When you help each other, you help yourselves.

remember...

Together, you and your co-workers make your organization succeed.

YOUR
MARKETPLACE

... is unlimited

#5 Your Marketplace

definition

Your Marketplace is the area in which you sell, and in which your clients and prospective customers buy. Its only boundaries are those imposed by you and your ability to communicate.

what to do

Your marketplace should be protected, developed, and expanded. Protect it by providing better products and service than your competitors. Develop and expand it through prospecting, marketing, and self-promotion.

why to do it

Success breeds success. Being visible, proactive, and successful in your existing marketplace reassures your clients that doing business with you is the right decision. It helps you gain new customers and enhance your company's profits.

remember...

Your marketplace can extend as far as your company can reach.

REPUTATIONS

... endure

#6 Reputations

definition

Your Reputation is what other people say about you, your organization or company, its products, or its service. People in your marketplace know you by reputation – even before they do business with you.

what to do

Believe in your work, do it well, and be proud of what you do. Speak highly of your organization and your co-workers, and ask your clients to spread the good word about doing business with you.

why to do it

A good reputation is one of the most powerful marketing devices of all: it brings in many clients, creates positive expectations, and leads to much profitable business.

remember...

A good reputation brings in business; a bad one drives it away.

Water Cooler Wisdom

50 Quick Tips For Workplace Success!

Knowing Your Organization

Workbook

General Instructions:

Refer to "Using the Workbooks in *Water Cooler Wisdom*" on page 1. Now (re)read the **Knowing Your Organization** section of *Water Cooler Wisdom.* Reflect on each Quick-Tip as you read it. Think about your company or organization, your marketplace, your clients, your vendors, your co-workers, your manager and your own performance. Ask yourself how you, your company and others you work with ought to perform in this area. Note what things are going really well. Also make note of where things can improve. Ask yourself what can be done to achieve better results. What should the company do? What should your manager do? What should your co-workers do? What should you do? Off-the-cuff answers might help a little but won't offer you or your organization the same benefit as more deeply thought out ideas. Be sure to apply your most considered suggestions to the four exercises that follow.

Exercise One:

1. Think about the six Quick-Tips in the **Knowing Your Organization** section. Select one of the six Quick-Tips that you think your company or organization is most successful at. Write the Quick-Tip name and number on the line below.

_____

Quick-Tip Name and #

2. Why is your organization so successful in this area?

_____

_____

_____

_____

_____

3. How and where can this success be duplicated in other areas of your company or organization?

_____

_____

_____

_____

_____

4. What would the benefits be to the organization as a whole if this success were duplicated?

_____

_____

_____

_____

_____

Exercise Two:

Please review the six Quick-Tips from **Knowing Your Organization** again before continuing. For this exercise, you will be asked to identify up to three Quick-Tips from this section that address areas where you believe your company or organization can make improvements. Later, you will be asked to select one Quick-Tip to use in an exercise called Stop, Start, Continue, and subsequently answer the nine open-ended questions.

5. Identify up to three Quick-Tips that represent areas where your company or organization may need improvement, or, to put it another way, the Quick-Tips that your company or organization could be more successful at. List the name and Quick-Tip number of the one you feel is most important on line "a," the second most important on line "b," and the third most important on line "c."

a)_____

b)_____

c)_____

6. For the next set of questions, please refer only to Quick-Tip "a," and once again fill in the Quick-Tip number and name below.

a)_____

7. Now think about Quick-Tip "a" carefully. Consider how your company or organization is currently performing in this area. Think about its relationships with others (such as employees, stockholders, customers, clients, prospects, vendors, etc.). Ask yourself how your company or organization can improve in this area.

Exercise Three:

Again, consider only Quick-Tip "a." In this exercise you will be using the Stop, Start, Continue model and asked to think specifically and critically about Quick-Tip "a." You will make three lists in this exercise:

- In the left column (Stop), you will identify and list what should stop taking place for your company or organization to be more successful with regard to Quick-Tip "a."
- In the middle column (Start), you will identify and list what must begin taking place in order to improve performance with regard to Quick-Tip "a."
- In the right column (Continue), you will identify and list things that are successful and should continue to be done with regard to Quick-Tip "a."

An example of a partially filled out Stop, Start, Continue grid:

What should your organization stop, start, and continue so it is more successful regarding:

_____*Your Manager - #3*_____?

Quick-Tip "a," Name & #

STOP	START	CONTINUE
handing out work without enough information to do a thorough job	telling someone when you are in and out of the building so we know where you are	telling us when we do a good job
expecting last-minute overtime without enough time to make arrangements with and for our families	having more time to listen to our concerns	asking our opinion

8. Now, please fill in Quick-Tip "a" on the line provided in the grid below. Then proceed to fill in the grid by continually thinking about Quick-Tip "a" and detailing what your organization should stop, start, and continue so it will be more successful in the area of Quick-Tip "a."

What should your organization stop, start, and continue so it is more successful regarding: _____? *Quick-Tip "a," Name & #*		
STOP	START	CONTINUE

Exercise Four:

Answer the following nine open-ended questions.

9. Considering the suggestions you made above, what is the one most important improvement that should be made regarding Quick-Tip "a"?

_____

_____

_____

_____

_____

_____

10. Why do you believe it is most important?

_____

_____

_____

_____

_____

11. What are the benefits to your company or organization, employees, customers, vendors, associates, etc. of having this improvement in place? (Be specific – give details.)

_____

_____

_____

_____

_____

12. How would you implement this new improvement? (Be specific – give details.)

_____

_____

_____

_____

_____

_____

_____

13. What obstacles are in the way of doing this successfully? (Be specific.)

_____

_____

_____

_____

_____

_____

_____

14. How would you remove these obstacles? (Be specific.)

_____

_____

_____

_____

_____

_____

_____

15. What do you need personally, to improve your own performance in this area?

_____

_____

_____

_____

_____

_____

16. What would be the first steps to begin implementing this
improvement? (Be specific.)

_____

_____

_____

_____

_____

_____

17. Other comments.

_____

_____

_____

_____

_____

_____

Additional Exercises:
To explore improvements in any or all of the other five Quick-
Tip areas from **Knowing Your Organization**, simply repeat this
procedure using additional paper.

Notes

Developing Sales

If you want to excel in a highly aggressive marketplace – whether you provide services, products, or both – selling with integrity is essential. Successful selling is based on using top-level skill within quality relationships. Developing successful relationships is what *Water Cooler Wisdom* is all about. The following five Quick-Tips show key perspectives on sales and a professional approach for turning customers into clients.

SELLING

... is based on relationships

#7 Selling

definition

Selling means creating a willingness in your client to buy from you.

what to do

Selling involves more than just your tangible products or service. It involves how your client feels about the way you do business together. To sell effectively, you must provide professional behavior and service, ask questions, listen, and focus on satisfying your client's needs.

why to do it

Every client's preference is to do business where they feel comfortable, understood, and important. Offering that sort of business relationship is the most important sale of all.

remember...

Your successful relationships with clients will create sales for you and your company.

BUYING
DECISIONS
... are your clients' solutions

#8 Buying Decisions

definition

Buying Decisions are the choices to purchase. They're made when a client's buying criteria are satisfactorily met.

what to do

If you can demonstrate that your product will satisfy your client's needs, then your client will buy. Help your clients identify their needs: what they want, why they want it, how they will use it, how it will help them, and how having it will make them feel. Then show them how your product or service satisfies those needs.

why to do it

People buy for their reasons, not yours. Until they know clearly what those reasons are – and how your product addresses them – they will not buy from you. When they do know clearly, buying decisions are more easily and appropriately made.

remember...

An appropriate buying decision makes a client happy; an inappropriate one can be a lingering problem.

CLOSING
THE SALE
... earns you the prize

Closing
The Sale

definition

Closing the Sale is when you ask your customer to reach a final buying decision. To do it successfully, you must gain clarity and agreement from the customer through every step of the sales process.

what to do

Begin the selling process by establishing rapport. Ask the customer what his or her needs are, and listen to the response. Describe the ways your product will satisfy this customer's needs, and finally ask them to buy from you. Address objections, and again ask the customer to buy.

why to do it

Asking customers to buy from you is the key to closing sales. Establishing open rapport with customers makes the asking easy and natural; creating the opportunity to ask several times increases your chance of success.

remember...

Closing the sale helps your customer, your company, and yourself.

REFERRALS

... are your easiest sales

#10 Referrals

definition

A Referral is a potential customer who is recommended to you or your company by another person.

what to do

Follow up with your clients by asking them for referrals on a regular basis; if you have earned your clients' respect and trust, they will help you. Always contact the referrals whose names you receive, and always thank the clients who referred them to you.

why to do it

Doing business with referrals makes your job easier: referred customers are more trusting, cooperative, and quicker to purchase than customers whom you have not yet met. Referrals help you and your organization build and maintain a strong network and client base.

remember...

Favorable referrals deliver business; unfavorable ones drive it away.

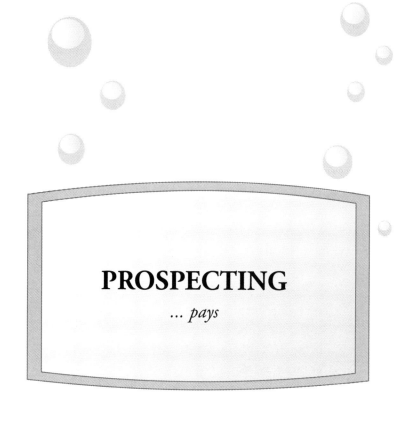

PROSPECTING

... pays

#11 Prospecting

definition

Prospecting is increasing your business by proactively seeking out new customers and opportunities.

what to do

Do your work in a way that makes you proud, and tell people about it. Develop a realistic prospecting plan and follow it faithfully. Contact prospects consistently in ways appropriate to your organization, and ask them to do business with you when they become ready.

why to do it

Actively prospecting allows you to reach more buyers, earn more sales, be more productive, and use your time efficiently during slow periods.

remember...

Prospecting isn't nearly as hard as waiting around for something to do.

Water Cooler **Wisdom**

50 Quick Tips For Workplace Success!

Developing Sales

Workbook

General Instructions:

Refer to "Using the Workbooks in *Water Cooler Wisdom*" on page 1. Now (re)read the **Developing Sales** section of *Water Cooler Wisdom*. Reflect on each Quick-Tip as you read it. Think about your company or organization, your marketplace, your clients, your vendors, your co-workers, your manager and your own performance. Ask yourself how you, your company and others you work with ought to perform in this area. Note what things are going really well. Also make note of where things can improve. Ask yourself what can be done to achieve better results. What should the company do? What should your manager do? What should your co-workers do? What should you do? Off-the-cuff answers might help a little but won't offer you or your organization the same benefit as more deeply thought out ideas. Be sure to apply your most considered suggestions to the four exercises that follow.

Exercise One:

1. Think about the five Quick-Tips in the **Developing Sales** section. Select one of the five Quick-Tips that you think your company or organization is most successful at. Write the Quick-Tip name and number on the line below.

_____

Quick-Tip Name and #

2. Why is your organization so successful in this area?

_____

_____

_____

_____

_____

3. How and where can this success be duplicated in other areas of your company or organization?

_____

_____

_____

_____

_____

4. What would the benefits be to the organization as a whole if this success were duplicated?

_____

_____

_____

_____

_____

Exercise Two:

Please review the five Quick-Tips from **Developing Sales** again before continuing. For this exercise, you will be asked to identify up to three Quick-Tips from this section that address areas where you believe your company or organization can make improvements. Later, you will be asked to select one Quick-Tip to use in an exercise called Stop, Start, Continue, and subsequently answer the nine open-ended questions.

5. Identify up to three Quick-Tips that represent areas where your company or organization may need improvement, or, to put it another way, the Quick-Tips that your company or organization could be more successful at. List the name and Quick-Tip number of the one you feel is most important on line "a," the second most important on line "b," and the third most important on line "c."

a)_____

b)_____

c)_____

6. For the next set of questions, please refer only to Quick-Tip "a," and once again fill in the Quick-Tip number and name below.

a)_____

7. Now think about Quick-Tip "a" carefully. Consider how your company or organization is currently performing in this area. Think about its relationships with others (such as employees, stockholders, customers, clients, prospects, vendors, etc.). Ask yourself how your company or organization can improve in this area.

Exercise Three:

Again, consider only Quick-Tip "a." In this exercise you will be using the Stop, Start, Continue model and asked to think specifically and critically about Quick-Tip "a." You will make three lists in this exercise:

- In the left column (Stop), you will identify and list what should stop taking place for your company or organization to be more successful with regard to Quick-Tip "a."
- In the middle column (Start), you will identify and list what must begin taking place in order to improve performance with regard to Quick-Tip "a."
- In the right column (Continue), you will identify and list things that are successful and should continue to be done with regard to Quick-Tip "a."

**An example of a partially filled out
Stop, Start, Continue grid:**

What should your organization stop, start, and continue so it is more successful regarding: _Closing the Sale - #9_ ? *Quick-Tip "a," Name & #*		
STOP	START	CONTINUE
thinking the competition is better than us	training us more in closing techniques	providing great after-sale service
having unreachable sales quotas		researching our clients needs

8. Now, please fill in Quick-Tip "a" on the line provided in the grid below. Then proceed to fill in the grid by continually thinking about Quick-Tip "a" and detailing what your organization should stop, start, and continue so it will be more successful in the area of Quick-Tip "a."

What should your organization stop, start, and continue so it is more successful regarding:		
_____?		
Quick-Tip "a," Name & #		
STOP	START	CONTINUE

Exercise Four:

Answer the following nine open-ended questions.

9. Considering the suggestions you made above, what is the one most important improvement that should be made regarding Quick-Tip "a"?

_____

_____

_____

_____

_____

_____

10. Why do you believe it is most important?

_____

_____

_____

_____

_____

_____

11. What are the benefits to your company or organization, employees, customers, vendors, associates, etc. of having this improvement in place? (Be specific – give details.)

_____

_____

_____

_____

_____

_____

12. How would you implement this new improvement?
(Be specific – give details.)

_____

_____

_____

_____

_____

_____

13. What obstacles are in the way of doing this successfully?
(Be specific.)

_____

_____

_____

_____

_____

_____

14. How would you remove these obstacles? (Be specific.)

_____

_____

_____

_____

_____

_____

15. What do you need personally, to improve your own performance in this area?

_____

_____

_____

_____

_____

_____

16. What would be the first steps to begin implementing this
improvement? (Be specific.)

_____

_____

_____

_____

_____

_____

17. Other comments.

_____

_____

_____

_____

_____

_____

Additional Exercises:

To explore improvements in any or all of the other four Quick-
Tip areas from **Developing Sales,** simply repeat this procedure
using additional paper.

Notes

Customer Service That Works

Today's marketplace is crowded and competitive, driving even the most successful organizations to excel at their service relationships. Increasingly discerning customers continue to raise the bar of acceptable service. Customers need to be heard, understood, appreciated, and given good value in exchange for their hard-earned dollars in order for you to win at customer service. Putting the next group of Quick-Tips to use will help you provide the customer service that leads to client loyalty.

CUSTOMER
SERVICE

... matters

#12 Customer Service

definition

Customer Service is how you communicate with your clients as people, meet their needs and expectations, and keep your word. It means supporting your clients in the ways that satisfy them.

what to do

Serve each client "givingly," by adopting their best interests as your best interests. Appear happy to help, be proactive, and always do more than your clients expect. Leave nothing half-done – see every task through to successful completion.

why to do it

The quality of customer service is measured entirely by the client. Clients who receive great service will be more satisfied with your company and its products, happier with their decision to do business with you, and more likely to buy from you again. They'll also be far more cooperative in solving problems that arise.

remember...

*The only customer service that helps your business is **great** customer service.*

CUSTOMERS

... pay your wage

#**13** Customers

definition

Customers are buyers who purchase or use your business's products or services for the first time. When they buy repeatedly, customers become clients.

what to do

If you think of each customer as providing your pay-check, every customer's importance immediately becomes clear. Your goal is to turn every customer into a repeat-business client. To do that, you must provide every customer with top-notch treatment from the moment you meet – even before they buy.

why to do it

Your opportunity to create a long-term business relationship with your customers begins before the first sale – even before they measure the value of your product or service. It begins with your first contact, when they decide how they feel about doing business with you.

remember...

Dissatisfied customers take their business elsewhere. And part of your paycheck goes with them.

CLIENTS

... are for keeping

#14 Clients

definition

Clients are customers who decide to do business with you repeatedly. A relationship has developed – it must be actively and professionally maintained.

what to do

If you think of your clients as you do your friends, your willingness to help them will become automatic. Treat them with kindness and respect as you maintain ongoing contact, follow up on purchases, and ask for feedback and referrals. Above all, keep their best interests in mind.

why to do it

Clients do business with people who make them feel good. Clients are looking for pleasurable, productive, profitable, long-lasting relationships.

remember...

Your good relationship with your client is the hardest thing for a competitor to outdo.

CUSTOMER SATISFACTION
... means success

#15 Customer Satisfaction

definition

True Customer Satisfaction occurs when your customer is sincerely pleased with you, your organization, your products, and your service.

what to do

Imagine that you come to work just to help each individual customer. Be gracious and sincere, and support your customer in the ways he or she needs. If you remember that everything you do to please your customer ultimately contributes to your paycheck, you'll want to do even more than the customer expects.

why to do it

When your customers are satisfied, they keep doing business with you. As their satisfaction increases, they become more and more trusting. Future transactions become easier, and working with them becomes more enjoyable and more rewarding.

remember...

If your customers are satisfied, it means that you are doing your job well.

FOLLOW UP

... to stay in control

#16 Follow Up

definition

Following Up is maintaining ongoing communication with your clients after the initial contact or sale. It's the best tactic for effective customer service, client retention, and prospecting.

what to do

Follow up frequently after each sale, making sure that each contact is made for a specific reason, and to accomplish a specific goal. For example, contact your clients to request an evaluation of your product or service, to seek referrals, or to thank them.

why to do it

Your clients measure the quality of your business relationship. By following up and communicating regularly, you reassure them that working with you continues to be the right business choice.

remember...

Your clients are often contacted by your competitors; shouldn't they hear more often from you?

CLIENT
LOYALTY

... is up to you

#17 Client Loyalty

definition

Client Loyalty is a faithful, powerful allegiance your clients feel to you, your organization, its products, and its service. Loyal clients are easier to serve and satisfy.

what to do

Build loyalty by delivering great service in whatever way is most meaningful to each client. Be sincere, patient, helpful, and friendly. And always do business with total integrity.

why to do it

Loyal clients provide greater financial rewards for your organization; they create a strong base of business, and help ensure your paycheck. When you know that you have truly helped your clients and nurtured their loyalty, everything about your work feels more worthwhile.

remember...

Client loyalty is built over time; it is maintained by the work you do.

Water Cooler Wisdom

50 Quick Tips For Workplace Success!

Customer Service That Works

Workbook

General Instructions:

Refer to "Using the Workbooks in *Water Cooler Wisdom*" on page 1. Now (re)read the **Customer Service That Works** section of *Water Cooler Wisdom*. Reflect on each Quick-Tip as you read it. Think about your company or organization, your marketplace, your clients, your vendors, your co-workers, your manager and your own performance. Ask yourself how you, your company and others you work with ought to perform in this area. Note what things are going really well. Also make note of where things can improve. Ask yourself what can be done to achieve better results. What should the company do? What should your manager do? What should your co-workers do? What should you do? Off-the-cuff answers might help a little but won't offer you or your organization the same benefit as more deeply thought out ideas. Be sure to apply your most considered suggestions to the four exercises that follow.

Exercise One:

1. Think about the six Quick-Tips in the **Customer Service That Works** section. Select one of the six Quick-Tips that you think your company or organization is most successful at. Write the Quick-Tip name and number on the line below.

_____

Quick-Tip Name and #

2. Why is your organization so successful in this area?

_____

_____

_____

_____

_____

3. How and where can this success be duplicated in other areas of your company or organization?

_____

_____

_____

_____

4. What would the benefits be to the organization as a whole if this success were duplicated?

_____

_____

_____

_____

_____

Exercise Two:

Please review the six Quick-Tips from the **Customer Service That Works** section again before continuing. For this exercise, you will be asked to identify up to three Quick-Tips from this section that address areas where you believe your company or organization can make improvements. Later, you will be asked to select one Quick-Tip to use in an exercise called Stop, Start, Continue, and subsequently answer the nine open-ended questions.

5. Identify up to three Quick-Tips that represent areas where your company or organization may need improvement, or, to put it another way, the Quick-Tips that your company or organization could be more successful at. List the name and Quick-Tip number of the one you feel is most important on line "a," the second most important on line "b," and the third most important on line "c."

    a)_____

    b)_____

    c)_____

6. For the next set of questions, please refer only to Quick-Tip "a," and once again fill in the Quick-Tip number and name below.

    a)_____

7. Now think about Quick-Tip "a" carefully. Consider how your company or organization is currently performing in this area. Think about its relationships with others (such as employees, stockholders, customers, clients, prospects, vendors, etc.). Ask yourself how your company or organization can improve in this area.

Exercise Three:

Again, consider only Quick-Tip "a." In this exercise you will be using the Stop, Start, Continue model and asked to think specifically and critically about Quick-Tip "a." You will make three lists in this exercise:

- In the left column (Stop), you will identify and list what should stop taking place for your company or organization to be more successful with regard to Quick-Tip "a."
- In the middle column (Start), you will identify and list what must begin taking place in order to improve performance with regard to Quick-Tip "a."
- In the right column (Continue), you will identify and list things that are successful and should continue to be done with regard to Quick-Tip "a."

**An example of a partially filled out
Stop, Start, Continue grid:**

What should your organization stop, start, and continue so it is more successful regarding: _Customer Satisfaction - #15_ ?		
Quick-Tip "a," Name & #		
STOP	START	CONTINUE
speaking negatively about our customers	doing it right the first time	customer satisfaction surveys
ignoring problems – deal with them immediately	an employee focus group to improve service	

8. Now, please fill in Quick-Tip "a" on the line provided in the grid below. Then proceed to fill in the grid by continually thinking about Quick-Tip "a" and detailing what your organization should stop, start, and continue so it will be more successful in the area of Quick-Tip "a."

What should your organization stop, start, and continue so it is more successful regarding: _____? *Quick-Tip "a," Name & #*		
STOP	START	CONTINUE

Exercise Four:

Answer the following nine open-ended questions.

9. Considering the suggestions you made above, what is the one most important improvement that should be made regarding Quick-Tip "a"?

_____

_____

_____

_____

_____

_____

10. Why do you believe it is most important?

_____

_____

_____

_____

_____

11. What are the benefits to your company or organization, employees, customers, vendors, associates, etc. of having this improvement in place? (Be specific – give details.)

_____

_____

_____

_____

_____

_____

12. How would you implement this new improvement? (Be specific – give details.)

_____

_____

_____

_____

_____

_____

13. What obstacles are in the way of doing this successfully? (Be specific.)

_____

_____

_____

_____

_____

_____

14. How would you remove these obstacles? (Be specific.)

_____

_____

_____

_____

_____

_____

15. What do you need personally, to improve your own performance in this area?

_____

_____

_____

_____

_____

_____

16. What would be the first steps to begin implementing this improvement? (Be specific.)

_____

_____

_____

_____

_____

17. Other comments.

_____

_____

_____

_____

_____

Additional Exercises:
To explore improvements in any or all of the other five Quick-Tip areas from **Customer Service That Works,** simply repeat this procedure using additional paper.

Notes

Communicating Effectively

Communication defines relationship potential both at and away from work. People choose to associate with those they like – people they can relate to – people who relate to them. When you communicate effectively you increase the strength of your customer relationships, increase your client base, and increase the potential to do even more business with the clients you already have. Read the Quick-Tips in this section and see how you can become an even more successful communicator.

RAPPORT

... creates successful relationships

#18 Rapport

definition

Rapport is a mutually clear and comfortable feeling between two people; good rapport means a relationship is in harmony.

what to do

First, be open and giving of yourself. Then, focus on the person you're communicating with, and help them feel important: maintain eye contact, smile, listen, and be patient. Appreciate people for who they are, and care about what they have to say. Be willing to look at things from their point of view.

why to do it

Establishing rapport makes communication easier, more trusting, flexible, dependable, and productive. Enhancing rapport strengthens relationships, and encourages more ambitious and substantial accomplishments.

remember...

Rapport allows people to move together toward their goals.

EFFECTIVE
COMMUNICATION
... reaches your target

#19 Effective Communication

definition

Effective Communication occurs when your message is received and understood. It has two parts: the content of the message, and the way your client feels about you and the way you deliver it.

what to do

Speak to all your clients in terms they understand; listen and respond sincerely. Ask questions, maintain eye contact, be patient and still. Speak their names, smile, be friendly and straightforward. If you have a genuine interest in your clients, you will become the reason they want to do business with your company.

why to do it

Effective communication gets your message across clearly and paves the way for successful business transactions and relationships. It makes clients feel comfortable, and is vital for client retention. Ineffective communication limits transactions and relationships to less than their full potential value.

remember...

Effective communication delivers the message to your client; ineffective communication delivers your client to your competitor.

THE TELEPHONE

... gets your message across

#20 The Telephone

definition

The Telephone is a powerful and readily accessible communication tool. Use it skillfully, and you can gather and distribute information, make sales, and service your clients.

what to do

When you're on the phone, listen to the other person, ask questions, and respond sincerely with the intention of being helpful. It's important to feel and sound warm; smiling as you speak will help you do that.

why to do it

People like to be listened to and appreciated. The better you listen and the friendlier you sound on the telephone, the more likely it is you will receive cooperation and good results.

remember...

Poor telephone communication is like a bad connection: your message never gets through.

THANK YOU

... is more than words

#21 Thank You

definition

Thank You is a sincere expression of heartfelt appreciation.

what to do

When you thank someone, make eye contact, smile, and let your feelings of warmth and gratitude clearly come through.

why to do it

Before almost anything else, people evaluate how they feel about doing business with you. When you give a sincere thank you, you make someone feel good: they get the message that you appreciate their actions – and the feeling that you appreciate them. An insincere thank you, on the other hand, feels like a dismissal, and gives the message "good-bye."

remember...

Say thank you when you mean it, and mean it when you say it.

Water Cooler **Wisdom**

50 Quick Tips For Workplace Success!

Communicating Effectively

Workbook

General Instructions:

Refer to "Using the Workbooks in *Water Cooler Wisdom*" on page 1. Now (re)read the **Communicating Effectively** section of *Water Cooler Wisdom*. Reflect on each Quick-Tip as you read it. Think about your own performance. Review how your performance relates to your company or organization, your marketplace, your clients, your vendors, your co-workers, and your manager. Ask yourself how you ought to perform in this area. Note your strengths – things that are going really well. Also make note of where things can improve. Ask yourself what can be done to achieve better results. What should the company do? What should your manager do? What should your co-workers do? What should you do? Off-the-cuff answers might help a little but won't offer you or your organization the same benefit as more deeply thought out ideas. Be sure to apply your most considered suggestions to the four exercises that follow.

Exercise One:

1. Think about the four Quick-Tips in the **Communicating Effectively** section. Select one of the four Quick-Tips that you think you are most successful at. Write the Quick-Tip name and number on the line below.

_____

Quick-Tip Name and #

2. Why are you so successful in this area?

_____

_____

_____

_____

_____

3. How can you use this strength to help improve other areas of your company or organization?

_____

_____

_____

_____

4. What would the benefits be to the organization as a whole if you were successful at making these improvements?

_____

_____

_____

_____

Exercise Two:

Please review the four Quick-Tips from **Communicating Effectively** again before continuing. For this exercise, you will be asked to identify up to three Quick-Tips from this section that address areas where you believe you can make improvements. Later, you will be asked to select one Quick-Tip to use in an exercise called Stop, Start, Continue, and subsequently answer the nine open-ended questions.

5. Identify up to three Quick-Tips that represent areas where you may need improvement, or, to put it another way, the Quick-Tips that could help you be more successful. List the name and Quick-Tip number of the one you feel is most important on line "a," the second most important on line "b," and the third most important on line "c."

a)_____

b)_____

c)_____

6. For the next set of questions, please refer only to Quick-Tip "a," and once again fill in the Quick-Tip number and name below.

a)_____

7. Now think about Quick-Tip "a" carefully. Consider how you are currently performing in this area. Think about your relationship with others (such as employees, stockholders, customers, clients, prospects, vendors, etc.). Again, ask yourself how you can improve in this area.

Exercise Three:

Consider only Quick-Tip "a." In this exercise you will be using the Stop, Start, Continue model and asked to think specifically and critically about Quick-Tip "a." You will make three lists in this exercise:

- In the left column (Stop), you will identify and list what you should stop doing to be more successful with regard to Quick-Tip "a."
- In the middle column (Start), you will identify and list what you must begin doing in order to improve your performance with regard to Quick-Tip "a."
- In the right column (Continue), you will identify and list things that you are successful at and should continue doing with regard to Quick-Tip "a."

An example of a partially filled out Stop, Start, Continue grid:

What should you personally stop, start, and continue so you are more successful regarding: _The Telephone, #20_ ? _Quick-Tip "a," Name & #_		
STOP	START	CONTINUE
seeming like I am in a hurry when others call for information	changing my voice mail message every day so people know if I am in the office	returning calls on time so people don't need to call me back as often, leaving me more time to do my other work
interrupting people when they are talking to me	answering within the first two rings when possible	smiling while I am on the phone, using a pleasant voice

8. Now, please fill in Quick-Tip "a" on the line provided in the grid below. Then proceed to fill in the grid by continually thinking about Quick-Tip "a" and detailing what you should stop, start, and continue so you will be more successful in the area of Quick-Tip "a."

What should you personally stop, start, and continue so you are more successful regarding: _____? *Quick-Tip "a," Name & #*		
STOP	START	CONTINUE

Exercise Four:

Answer the following nine open-ended questions.

9. Considering the suggestions you made above, what is the one most important improvement you can make regarding Quick-Tip "a"?

_____

_____

_____

_____

_____

_____

10. Why do you believe it is most important?

_____

_____

_____

_____

_____

11. What are the benefits to yourself, your company or organization, employees, customers, vendors, associates, etc. of having this improvement in place? (Be specific – give details.)

_____

_____

_____

_____

_____

12. How will you implement this new improvement?
(Be specific – give details.)

_____

_____

_____

_____

_____

_____

_____

13. What obstacles are in the way of doing this successfully?
(Be specific.)

_____

_____

_____

_____

_____

_____

_____

14. How would you remove these obstacles? (Be specific.)

_____

_____

_____

_____

_____

_____

_____

15. What do you think the benefits of making this improvement will be in your personal life outside the workplace? (Be specific.)

_____

_____

_____

_____

_____

16. Who will benefit from these improvements taking place? (Be specific.)

_____

_____

_____

_____

_____

17. Other comments.

_____

_____

_____

_____

_____

Additional Exercises:
To explore improvements in any or all of the other three Quick-Tip areas from **Communicating Effectively,** simply repeat this procedure using additional paper.

Notes

Becoming More Productive

Most people already work hard. Becoming more productive is about working smarter – not harder. It's about increasing your knowledge, work output and quality. It's about being more efficient and more effective. It's about having a simple, strategic approach to your work and the discipline to carry it out. Quick-Tips #22 - #27 will help you increase your work output and quality, thereby increasing your value to your organization.

PUNCTUALITY

... says you care

#22 Punctuality

definition

Punctuality means being physically and attitudinally on time and prepared. It is a habit of successful people.

what to do

Arrive at work early enough to prepare yourself for the day. Plan how you can best help your business and clients, set your work goals, and begin on time. Be punctual for all meetings, appointments, and deadlines.

why to do it

Being punctual demonstrates respect for your co-workers and clients, and pride in yourself. Completing your assignments punctually contributes to efficient output. You will be noticed, appreciated, and rewarded for your dependability and good attitude; others will follow. You and your entire organization will benefit.

remember...

Being punctual demonstrates your commitment to your company's success.

ASK QUESTIONS

... and get answers

#23 Ask Questions

definition

Asking Questions is the way to gain the information and understanding necessary to create solutions.

what to do

Ask open-ended questions in a pleasant, direct manner; listen non-judgmentally to the responses. People will tell you what you want and need to know.

why to do it

When you ask people questions, you demonstrate that you care about them and what they have to say. You help them feel good about themselves – and about you. Asking questions of your clients and co-workers helps you establish rapport, and strengthens your relationships; it's also the best way to learn exactly how to help people most effectively.

remember...

Asking questions is the first step to greater wisdom.

DELEGATE

... to accomplish more

#24 Delegate

definition

When you Delegate, you assign a task to someone else, while maintaining responsibility for its successful completion.

what to do

Assign people tasks they are capable of accomplishing. Give people clear, detailed instructions of what you expect, and be certain they understand. Then support them as needed and be available to guide them.

why to do it

When you delegate successfully, you greatly increase your own output – while allowing others to gain experience, confidence, and self-esteem.

remember...

When you delegate, you free your time, accomplish more, and help other workers grow.

SIMPLIFY

... and get more done

#25 Simplify

definition

To Simplify a task is to make it easier by breaking it down into small, manageable steps.

what to do

Identify the steps necessary to complete a large or complex task. One at a time, accomplish each step in productive sequence. Stay disciplined and focused on whichever step you're on, but always keep your desired final outcome in mind.

why to do it

Large challenges can be overwhelming, but when you reduce seemingly huge tasks to simpler components, you'll see that you can get each aspect of the job done right. You'll feel more self-confident, versatile, and skilled. You'll become significantly more productive.

remember...

Even the most complex task is simply a series of smaller steps.

PROACTIVITY

*... puts you in control, and
moves you ahead*

#26 Proactivity

definition

Proactivity is the creative process of anticipating, planning ahead and controlling a situation. The opposite of proactivity – reactivity – is reacting to a situation that's already out of your control.

what to do

Anticipate what's likely to happen next. Be creative, and imagine all the different actions you could take to affect that situation – and what the results of each possible action would be. Then choose and implement the action that will give you the results you want.

why to do it

When you keep the future impact of your actions in mind, it's easier to get good results – because the results are within your control. For example, work-loads are always easiest to handle when you manage them with forethought.

remember...

When you are aware of all the possibilities, it's easier to manage the outcome.

TRAINING

... is your opportunity to grow

#27 Training

definition

Training is the process that helps you perform with more understanding and greater expertise. Training gives you information, skill, experience, and wisdom. It is the activity that enables you to improve and grow.

what to do

Participate in the appropriate training opportunities that are offered to you, and request more as you feel the need. Approach each training session with an open mind and the determination to apply your new knowledge.

why to do it

Training is a privilege, the surest way to enhance your work and advance yourself. It allows you to demonstrate your best intentions and display your full worth.

remember...

Workers with training deserve and get more of what they want.

Water Cooler Wisdom

50 Quick Tips For Workplace Success!

Becoming More Productive

Workbook

General Instructions:

Refer to "Using the Workbooks in *Water Cooler Wisdom*" on page 1. Now (re)read the **Becoming More Productive** section of *Water Cooler Wisdom*. Reflect on each Quick-Tip as you read it. Think about your own performance. Review how your performance relates to your company or organization, your marketplace, your clients, your vendors, your co-workers, and your manager. Ask yourself how you ought to perform in this area. Note your strengths – things that are going really well. Also make note of where things can improve. Ask yourself what can be done to achieve better results. What should the company do? What should your manager do? What should your co-workers do? What should you do? Off-the-cuff answers might help a little but won't offer you or your organization the same benefit as more deeply thought out ideas. Be sure to apply your most considered suggestions to the four exercises that follow.

Exercise One:

1. Think about the six Quick-Tips in the **Becoming More Productive** section. Select one of the six Quick-Tips that you think you are most successful at. Write the Quick-Tip name and number on the line below.

_____

Quick-Tip Name and #

2. Why are you so successful in this area?

_____

_____

_____

_____

_____

3. How can you use this strength to help improve other areas of your company or organization?

_____

_____

_____

_____

_____

4. What would the benefits be to the organization as a whole if you were successful at making these improvements?

_____

_____

_____

_____

_____

Exercise Two:

Please review the four Quick-Tips from **Becoming More Productive** again before continuing. For this exercise, you will be asked to identify up to three Quick-Tips from this section that adress areas where you believe you can make improvements. Later, you will be asked to select one Quick-Tip to use in an exercise called Stop, Start, Continue, and subsequently answer the nine open-ended questions.

5. Identify up to three Quick-Tips that represent areas where you may need improvement, or, to put it another way, the Quick-Tips that could help you be more successful. List the name and Quick-Tip number of the one you feel is most important on line "a," the second most important on line "b," and the third most important on line "c."

a)_____

b)_____

c)_____

6. For the next set of questions, please refer only to Quick-Tip "a," and once again fill in the Quick-Tip number and name below.

a)_____

7. Now think about Quick-Tip "a" carefully. Consider how you are currently performing in this area. Think about your relationship with others (such as employees, stockholders, customers, clients, prospects, vendors, etc.). Again, ask yourself how you can improve in this area.

Exercise Three:

Consider only Quick-Tip "a." In this exercise you will be using the Stop, Start, Continue model and asked to think specifically and critically about Quick-Tip "a." You will make three lists in this exercise:

- In the left column (Stop), you will identify and list what you should stop doing to be more successful with regard to Quick-Tip "a."
- In the middle column (Start), you will identify and list what you must begin doing in order to improve your performance with regard to Quick-Tip "a."
- In the right column (Continue), you will identify and list things that you are successful at and should continue doing with regard to Quick-Tip "a."

**An example of a partially filled out
Stop, Start, Continue grid:**

What should you personally stop, start, and continue so you are more successful regarding: _____Delegate, #24_____ ? *Quick-Tip "a," Name & #*		
STOP	**START**	**CONTINUE**
delegating tasks at the last minute	delegating more often	providing all necessary information when I delegate
delegating to people who don't have time	being responsible for the work I delegate	

8. Now, please fill in Quick-Tip "a" on the line provided in the grid below. Then proceed to fill in the grid by continually thinking about Quick-Tip "a" and detailing what you should stop, start, and continue so you will be more successful in the area of Quick-Tip "a."

What should you personally stop, start, and continue so you are more successful regarding: _____? *Quick-Tip "a," Name & #*		
STOP	START	CONTINUE

Exercise Four:

Answer the following nine open-ended questions.

9. Considering the suggestions you made above, what is the one most important improvement you can make regarding Quick-Tip "a"?

_____

_____

_____

_____

_____

_____

10. Why do you believe it is most important?

_____

_____

_____

_____

_____

11. What are the benefits to yourself, your company or organization, employees, customers, vendors, associates, etc. of having this improvement in place? (Be specific – give details.)

_____

_____

_____

_____

_____

12. How will you implement this new improvement?
    (Be specific - give details.)

_____

_____

_____

_____

_____

_____

13. What obstacles are in the way of doing this successfully?
    (Be specific.)

_____

_____

_____

_____

_____

_____

14. How would you remove these obstacles? (Be specific.)

_____

_____

_____

_____

_____

15. What do you think the benefits of making this improvement will be in your personal life outside the workplace? (Be specific.)

_____

_____

_____

_____

_____

16. Who will benefit from these improvements taking place? (Be specific.)

_____

_____

_____

_____

17. Other comments.

_____

_____

_____

_____

Additional Exercises:
To explore improvements in any or all of the other five Quick-Tip areas from **Becoming More Productive**, simply repeat this procedure using additional paper.

Notes

Attitudes That Work

This section is downright personal. By applying these Quick-Tips you will be more successful at everything you do – in all aspects of business and life. With the right attitude, every relationship will change for the good. You will feel better about yourself. You will be a better employee, co-worker, or boss. Given that our thoughts guide our performance, remember this: When it comes to accomplishing anything, "whether you think you can (do it) or you think you can't (do it), you are probably right!"

HONESTY

... pays big dividends

#28 Honesty

definition

Honesty means being completely truthful – not trying to take advantage by giving partial information or being deceptive.

what to do

Keep the best interests of your client in mind, and be fair and honorable in all your dealings and transactions. Give your client all of the pertinent information – whether you are asked for it or not. Deliver everything you promise.

why to do it

When you are honest, you never have to hide from your clients or yourself. You gain the personal pride of knowing that you work with integrity. You gain the professional satisfaction of knowing that your clients can and do trust you. And you and your organization gain the profits of well-founded, long-lasting business relationships.

remember...

Honesty builds the most dependable and successful relationships.

MOTIVATION

... is the true reason within

#29 Motivation

definition

Your Motivation is what causes you to do what you do.

what to do

Do you work to make lots of money, help others, support a family, win praise, feel successful, take vacations...? Think about why you stay at this job; figure out what's really in it for you.

why to do it

Motivation guides your actions. By understanding what your motivation is, and by doing your job well, you can work more directly for what you truly want.

remember...

Motivation gives you the power to perform.

SELF-CONFIDENCE

... lets you reach your potential

#30 Self-Confidence

definition

Self-Confidence is the knowledge that you can do what you choose to do.

what to do

Believe in your ability to handle what comes your way, and then reach for what you want. Re-read your personal mission statement (see Quick-Tip #34), and take risks with the assurance that you are a strong, intelligent, and capable person.

why to do it

Your mind is your most powerful ally: believing that you can succeed allows you the opportunity to succeed. No matter what the outcome of your risk-taking, you'll gain information and experience, and keep moving forward.

remember...

With self-confidence, every challenge is an opportunity to look forward to.

PROFESSIONALISM

... is about standards

124
www.WaterCoolerWisdom.biz

Professionalism

definition

Professionalism means maintaining the highest standards of quality and ethics. A professional is knowledgeable, skilled, experienced, and up-to-date.

what to do

Always work at your best level. Keep current with all the new developments and information that are pertinent to your profession, train regularly, and improve constantly.

why to do it

Clients choose to do business with those who consistently deliver the highest-quality products and service in the most professional manner. Keep your standards at their peak, and your clients will continue to be satisfied.

remember...

Professionalism is your strongest contribution to your organization's continued good name.

GOALS
... give you purpose

#32 Goals

definition

Goals are what you set out to accomplish: clear visions with measurable attainment.

what to do

Decide exactly what you want to accomplish, and understand why. Outline a plan of small, simple steps you can take to accomplish your goals. Complete each step in turn. Be flexible enough to adjust for unforeseen problems or new information – but always work toward your ultimate goals.

why to do it

Goals give you a sense of purpose and power – because you choose them. Moving toward your goals in a series of small steps makes it easier for you to succeed, and easier to measure your progress; it allows you to savor the pride and satisfaction of your accomplishments along the way.

remember...

If you don't pursue goals, you'll always be where you are right now.

EXPERIENCE

... is the reward for time and effort

#33 Experience

definition

Experience is the familiarity, knowledge, and wisdom you gain with time.

what to do

Work hard to improve yourself and your performance, and make it your business to keep learning new things. Acknowledge and learn from all your accomplishments, and welcome the mistakes that teach you better ways.

why to do it

As you increase your familiarity, knowledge, and wisdom through experience, you'll be able to give more to your clients, your co-workers, and your employer. Your increased value will be recognized and rewarded.

remember...

Whether you succeed or fail, the experience you gain is always worthwhile.

A PERSONAL
MISSION STATEMENT

... reflects your standards

#34 A Personal Mission Statement

definition

A Personal Mission Statement describes the values, morals, and ethical standards you bring to your job.

what to do

Become aware of your reasons, motivations, and goals for working, and the standards by which you measure yourself. Write them all down. This is your personal mission statement. Look at it regularly, and remember why you're there.

why to do it

Having a personal mission statement helps you stay focused on your objectives and on what "doing a good job" means for you. It can give you the strength and clarity to get through difficult times on the job.

remember...

Understanding what's important to you keeps you headed in the right direction.

PERSEVERANCE

... keeps you moving ahead

#35 Perseverance

definition

Perseverance means continuing toward your goals despite difficulties and opposition.

what to do

Clearly identify your motivation and the goals you want to reach. Create a plan of simple steps to get you there, and complete each step in turn; change strategies as the need arises. Understand that over-coming discouragement is part of the process, and keep going anyway.

why to do it

With perseverance, you'll accomplish far more than the average worker. You'll discover that even the most difficult tasks can be completed successfully.

remember...

If you persevere, you'll most often reach your goal.

ADVICE

... is information to welcome and consider

#36 Advice

definition

Advice is a recommendation about an event, a condition, or an issue.

what to do

If your goal is to improve, advice is a strong ally. Consider all advice as valuable. Seek it out, listen with an open mind – and then make your own decisions.

why to do it

There are often several "right" ways to solve a problem. When you seek advice, you receive information and solutions you might not have thought of yourself. The more advice you get, the better your chances of finding and choosing the best solutions.

remember...

Gathering advice helps you discover new possibilities.

GROWTH

... promotes progress

#37 Growth

definition

Growth in an individual allows the expansion of skills, confidence, experience, output, and self-esteem. Growth in an organization allows the expansion of goals, market share, profits, reputation, and recognition.

what to do

The decision to grow personally – to improve – is entirely within your power. Set new goals for yourself, then persevere and work hard to achieve them. Look for new opportunities to learn, and accept new challenges.

why to do it

Growing as an individual – learning and accomplishing more – strengthens your pride and self-esteem. You become more valuable to yourself, and that increases your value to those around you. Rewards are sure to follow.

remember...

An organization can grow only as fast as the individuals who work there.

EXCEL

... and step ahead

#38 Excel

definition

To Excel means to out-perform yourself.

what to do

Learn more and do more. Search out ways to work smarter, more efficiently, faster, and more effectively. Approach your work with more pride and integrity. Do it better than you ever have before.

why to do it

The effort to excel helps you grow, feel better about yourself, and be worth more to your employer. You'll gain notice and recognition – and, in time, more personal and professional rewards.

remember...

The effort to excel rewards itself.

COMPETE

... to win

#39 Compete

definition

Competing is trying to be better, more efficient, and more effective than anyone else who does what you do.

what to do

The contest begins within yourself; be the absolute best you personally can be. Set the highest realistic standards and goals for yourself. Behave professionally, communicate effectively, and provide great customer service. Be persistent and visualize the winning results you expect.

why to do it

When you perform in a focused and competitive manner, you challenge yourself, expand your abilities, and produce the best results. With the best results, you'll earn the greatest rewards, and leave your competitors behind.

remember...

To win in business, you must out-perform those who are trying to improve on what you do.

SMILE

... it's an international language

#40 Smile

definition

A sincere Smile is when your lips curl up at the ends, your eyes get warm and relaxed, and you feel good inside.

what to do

When you interact with a client or a co-worker, imagine how pleased you'll feel when you help them. Now let those feelings shine through on your face, and be heard in your voice.

why to do it

A sincere smile opens the door to successful communication. It displays your good intentions, and puts other people at ease.

remember...

Business transactions that end with a smile usually begin with one.

SUCCESS

... means you've done it right

#41 Success

definition

Success is when you accomplish a goal that you've set for yourself.

what to do

Set clear goals and objectives for yourself. Write them down, create step-by-step plans to accomplish them, and follow through with perseverance and flexibility. Then, when you've accomplished a goal or objective to your satisfaction, step back and enjoy the feeling of success. Be proud – you've earned it.

why to do it

Success is a measure of a job well done, and nothing feels better.

remember...

Success is the fuel that powers your pride.

www.WaterCoolerWisdom.biz

Water Cooler Wisdom

50 Quick Tips For Workplace Success!

Attitudes That Work

Workbook

General Instructions:

Refer to "Using the Workbooks in *Water Cooler Wisdom*" on page 1. Now (re)read the **Attitudes That Work** section of *Water Cooler Wisdom*. Reflect on each Quick-Tip as you read it. Think about your own performance. Review how your performance relates to your company or organization, your marketplace, your clients, your vendors, your co-workers, and your manager. Ask yourself how you ought to perform in this area. Note your strengths – things that are going really well. Also make note of where things can improve. Ask yourself what can be done to achieve better results. What should the company do? What should your manager do? What should your co-workers do? What should you do? Off-the-cuff answers might help a little but won't offer you or your organization the same benefit as more deeply thought out ideas. Be sure to apply your most considered suggestions to the four exercises that follow.

Exercise One:

1. Think about the fourteen Quick-Tips in the **Attitudes That Work** section. Select one of the fourteen Quick-Tips that you think you are most successful at. Write the Quick-Tip name and number on the line below.

_____

Quick-Tip Name and #

2. Why are you so successful in this area?

_____

_____

_____

_____

_____

3. How can you use this strength to help improve other areas of your company or organization?

_____

_____

_____

_____

4. What would the benefits be to the organization as a whole if you were successful at making these improvements?

_____

_____

_____

_____

Exercise Two:

Please review the four Quick-Tips from **Attitudes That Work** again before continuing. For this exercise, you will be asked to identify up to three Quick-Tips from this section that address areas where you believe you can make improvements. Later, you will be asked to select one Quick-Tip to use in an exercise called Stop, Start, Continue, and subsequently answer the nine open-ended questions.

5. Identify up to three Quick-Tips that represent areas where you may need improvement, or, to put it another way, the Quick-Tips that could help you be more successful. List the name and Quick-Tip number of the one you feel is most important on line "a," the second most important on line "b," and the third most important on line "c."

a)_____

b)_____

c)_____

6. For the next set of questions, please refer only to Quick-Tip "a," and once again fill in the Quick-Tip number and name below.

a)_____

7. Now think about Quick-Tip "a" carefully. Consider how you are currently performing in this area. Think about your relationship with others (such as employees, stockholders, customers, clients, prospects, vendors, etc.). Again, ask yourself how you can improve in this area.

Exercise Three:

Consider only Quick-Tip "a." In this exercise you will be using the Stop, Start, Continue model and asked to think specifically and critically about Quick-Tip "a." You will make three lists in this exercise:

- In the left column (Stop), you will identify and list what you should stop doing to be more successful with regard to Quick-Tip "a."
- In the middle column (Start), you will identify and list what you must begin doing in order to improve your performance with regard to Quick-Tip "a."
- In the right column (Continue), you will identify and list things that you are successful at and should continue doing with regard to Quick-Tip "a."

An example of a partially filled out
Stop, Start, Continue grid:

What should you personally stop, start, and continue so you are more successful regarding:

Self-Confidence, #30 ?

Quick-Tip "a," Name & #

STOP	START	CONTINUE
telling myself that I can't do it	*believing in my abilities*	*trying to improve*
being afraid to take small risks	*asking for help to do things I don't know how to do*	

8. Now, please fill in Quick-Tip "a" on the line provided in the grid below. Then proceed to fill in the grid by continually thinking about Quick-Tip "a" and detailing what you should stop, start, and continue so you will be more successful in the area of Quick-Tip "a."

What should you personally stop, start, and continue so you are more successful regarding: _____? *Quick-Tip "a," Name & #*		
STOP	START	CONTINUE

Exercise Four:

Answer the following nine open-ended questions.

9. Considering the suggestions you made above, what is the one most important improvement you can make regarding Quick-Tip "a"?

_____

_____

_____

_____

_____

10. Why do you believe it is most important?

_____

_____

_____

_____

_____

11. What are the benefits to yourself, your company or organization, employees, customers, vendors, associates, etc. of having this improvement in place? (Be specific – give details.)

_____

_____

_____

_____

_____

12. How will you implement this new improvement?
(Be specific - give details.)

_____

_____

_____

_____

_____

_____

_____

13. What obstacles are in the way of doing this successfully?
(Be specific.)

_____

_____

_____

_____

_____

_____

_____

14. How would you remove these obstacles? (Be specific.)

_____

_____

_____

_____

_____

_____

_____

15. What do you think the benefits of making this improvement will be in your personal life outside the workplace? (Be specific.)

_____

_____

_____

_____

_____

16. Who will benefit from these improvements taking place? (Be specific.)

_____

_____

_____

_____

_____

17. Other comments.

_____

_____

_____

_____

_____

Additional Exercises:
To explore improvements in any or all of the other thirteen Quick-Tip areas from **Attitudes That Work,** simply repeat this procedure using additional paper.

Notes

Measuring and Analyzing Your Performance

Information relating to every aspect of your organization can be gathered, analyzed and measured. By becoming aware of what is going on with your business, department, or project early enough and with regularity, you can spot trends that can be guided to a more successful outcome. Analyze information in all areas of your organization. Seek input and listen to what your prospects, clients, vendors, co-workers, and competitors have to say. These nine Quick-Tips suggest why this input is important to your organization's bottom line.

SURVEY

... then you will know

#42 Survey

definition

To Survey is to gather and examine information from your clients and the marketplace about the perception of your company or organization, its products, or its performance.

what to do

Develop and implement a plan for systematically obtaining feedback, ideas, and suggestions from clients, consumers, co-workers, and others working in your industry and related fields. Interpret and analyze your findings. Then take steps – proactively – to improve on existing conditions, and prepare for the future.

why to do it

Business conditions change continually. Surveys provide information for anticipating and coping with change: they help you make adjustments that minimize losses and maximize opportunities. Surveys help you operate with more control, and limit unwanted risk.

remember...

Not surveying for information is a gamble: You can try your luck, but the odds are stacked against you.

TRENDS

... are undeniable

#43 Trends

definition

Trends are changes that can be measured or predicted in the performance of a person, business, or marketplace.

what to do

Measure your work performance regularly, and analyze how it is trending. When you see a trend in the right direction, be certain to support it. When you see a trend in the wrong direction, make appropriate corrections immediately.

why to do it

Small changes now can have a huge impact over the long term. By discovering trends early and making immediate small adjustments, you maximize opportunities and avoid having to make more difficult corrections when it may be too late.

remember...

Keep an eye on the trends, and you'll never be confronted with big surprises.

REPORTS
... point the way

#44 Reports

definition

Reports document the status of your business. They provide data you can analyze and use to spot trends.

what to do

Observe, document, and track every key aspect of your basic business activities; whenever possible, do it with numbers. Chart your progress, and analyze the results to identify trends in your business performance. Correct potential problems by making appropriate changes as soon as possible.

why to do it

When generated on a regular basis, reports allow you to inspect the elements of your business and document your progress. They help you discover problems early, when they are easiest to correct and when corrections will have the greatest long-term impact.

remember...

Reports are the road map of work; they show where you've been, and where you are going.

FEEDBACK

... tells it like it is

#45 Feedback

definition

Feedback is another person's assessment or response to what you do. Getting feedback is necessary for monitoring and strengthening your progress.

what to do

Ask people what they think – and they will tell you. Listen to what they say as objectively as possible, and analyze the information. Then, use what you learn to make whatever adjustments are appropriate.

why to do it

Business conditions and directions change continually; feedback gives you the information you need to stay on the right track. What's more, clients, co-workers, and others respect you when you ask for feedback. Asking people their opinions – and listening to the responses – strengthens the bonds between you.

remember...

Doing business without feedback is like flying blind without a compass: you're likely to head in the wrong direction.

QUALITY

... comes from you

#46 Quality

definition

Quality is the inherent integrity, reliability, and value of your products and service.

what to do

Create and maintain the highest possible quality in your products and service. Constantly evaluate them, and make sure that ongoing adjustments are part of your business plan. Stay alert: notice and communicate all opportunities for improvement.

why to do it

Clients expect and deserve superior quality. When you give your clients the best, they remain satisfied and loyal – the overall strength and potential for growth of your business or organization are enhanced.

remember...

Great quality satisfies your clients – and thwarts your competitors.

PROFITS

... are for you

#47 Profits

definition

Profits are the measurable financial gains that exist only when earnings exceed expenses.

what to do

Your job is to serve your clients at a profit to your company; to provide your clients with the best products and service in exchange for the best profit. Minimize expenses by working efficiently, reducing waste, and conserving resources.

why to do it

Profits allow your company to exist, and are the source of your paycheck. By doing everything you can to contribute to profits, you help give your company – and your job – a future.

remember...

For your job to continue, your company must make a profit.

CLIENT RETENTION

... is your business

#48 Client Retention

definition

Client Retention means continuing to do business with the clients you have.

what to do

To retain your clients, you must out-perform your competitors in service, product quality, value, ethics, and professionalism. It helps to remember that your clients provide your paycheck. Stay in touch with them. Ask them for suggestions about how you can improve - then do it. Do more than your clients expect. And above all, be sure to thank them.

why to do it

Retaining your clients makes your daily business operations more predictable and easier to manage. It requires less work and less expense to retain existing clients than it does to replace lost ones – and it's far more profitable.

remember...

A client who stays has value; a client who strays has none.

CLIENT EROSION

... costs you money

Client Erosion

definition

Client Erosion is a shrinkage in your number of clients. It means your business is going in the wrong direction.

what to do

To minimize client erosion, give your clients more of what they expect. Operate more professionally, and with more integrity. Provide better service. Outdo your competition. Do everything you can to enhance your client relationships (and in the process, you'll enhance the reputation of your organization). If clients stop doing business with you, talk with them and find out why – then make appropriate changes. Actively prospect for new clients.

why to do it

Replacing lost clients is harder, more expensive, and far less profitable than keeping the clients you already have.

remember...

It's easier to keep clients happy than it is to change their minds once they decide to leave.

THE BOTTOM LINE

... is a company's value

#50 The Bottom Line

definition

The Bottom Line is the amount of profit (or loss) a business makes overall – the dollars-and-cents accounting of total income and expenses.

what to do

To strengthen the overall bottom line, all employees must maximize the profitability of every element of the business. Each must work efficiently, use supplies and materials effectively, conserve energy resources, and look for ways to reduce costs.

why to do it

A business is only as strong as each of its component parts. For a company and its workers to earn the largest profits, every element of the business must be efficient and effective.

remember...

When the bottom line improves, everybody profits.

Water Cooler Wisdom

50 Quick Tips For Workplace Success!

Measuring and Analyzing Your Performance

Workbook

General Instructions:

Refer to "Using the Workbooks in *Water Cooler Wisdom*" on page 1. Now (re)read the **Measuring and Analyzing Your Performance** section of *Water Cooler Wisdom*. Reflect on each Quick-Tip as you read it. Think about your company or organization, your marketplace, your clients, your vendors, your co-workers, your manager and your own performance. Ask yourself how you, your company and others you work with ought to perform in this area. Note what things are going really well. Also make note of where things can improve. Ask yourself what can be done to achieve better results. What should the company do? What should your manager do? What should your co-workers do? What should you do? Off-the-cuff answers might help a little but won't offer you or your organization the same benefit as more deeply thought out ideas. Be sure to apply your most considered suggestions to the four exercises that follow.

Exercise One:

1. Think about the nine Quick-Tips in the **Measuring and Analyzing Your Performance** section. Select one of the nine Quick-Tips that you think your company or organization is most successful at. Write the Quick-Tip name and number on the line below.

_____

Quick-Tip Name and #

2. Why is your organization so successful in this area?

_____

_____

_____

_____

_____

3. How and where can this success be duplicated in other areas of your company or organization?

_____

_____

_____

_____

_____

4. What would the benefits be to the organization as a whole if this success were duplicated?

_____

_____

_____

_____

Exercise Two:

Please review the nine Quick-Tips from **Measuring and Analyzing Your Performance** again before continuing. For this exercise, you will be asked to identify up to three Quick-Tips from this section where you believe your company or organization can make improvements. Later, you will be asked to select one Quick-Tip to use in an exercise called Stop, Start, Continue, and subsequently answer the nine open-ended questions.

5. Identify up to three Quick-Tips that represent areas where your company or organization may need improvement, or, to put it another way, the Quick-Tips that your company or organization could be more successful at. List the name and Quick-Tip number of the one you feel is most important on line "a," the second most important on line "b," and the third most important on line "c."

a)_____

b)_____

c)_____

6. For the next set of questions, please refer only to Quick-Tip "a," and once again fill in the Quick-Tip number and name below.

a)_____

7. Now think about Quick-Tip "a" carefully. Consider how your company or organization is currently performing in this area. Think about its relationships with others (such as employees, stockholders, customers, clients, prospects, vendors, etc.). Ask yourself how your company or organization can improve in this area.

Exercise Three:

Again, consider only Quick-Tip "a." In this exercise you will be using the Stop, Start, Continue model and asked to think specifically and critically about Quick-Tip "a." You will make three lists in this exercise:

- In the left column (Stop), you will identify and list what should stop taking place for your company or organization to be more successful with regard to Quick-Tip "a."
- In the middle column (Start), you will identify and list what must begin taking place in order to improve performance with regard to Quick-Tip "a."
- In the right column (Continue), you will identify and list things that are successful and should continue to be done with regard to Quick-Tip "a."

An example of a partially filled out Stop, Start, Continue grid:

What should your organization stop, start, and continue so it is more successful regarding: Feedback, #45 ? Quick-Tip "a," Name & #		
STOP being closed-minded about suggestions	START actively asking for input	CONTINUE having a suggestion box
being to busy to listen	seeing all ideas as potentially valuable	

8. Now, please fill in Quick-Tip "a" on the line provided in the grid below. Then proceed to fill in the grid by continually thinking about Quick-Tip "a" and detailing what your organization should stop, start, and continue so it will be more successful in the area of Quick-Tip "a."

What should your organization stop, start, and continue so it is more successful regarding: _____?		
Quick-Tip "a," Name & #		
STOP	START	CONTINUE

Exercise Four:

Answer the following nine open-ended questions.

9. Considering the suggestions you made above, what is the one most important improvement that should be made regarding Quick-Tip "a"?

_____

_____

_____

_____

_____

_____

10. Why do you believe it is most important?

_____

_____

_____

_____

_____

11. What are the benefits to your company or organization, employees, customers, vendors, associates, etc. of having this improvement in place? (Be specific – give details.)

_____

_____

_____

_____

_____

12. How would you implement this new improvement? (Be specific – give details.)

_____

_____

_____

_____

_____

_____

13. What obstacles are in the way of doing this successfully? (Be specific.)

_____

_____

_____

_____

_____

_____

14. How would you remove these obstacles? (Be specific.)

_____

_____

_____

_____

_____

_____

15. What do you need personally, to improve your own performance in this area?

_____

_____

_____

_____

_____

_____

16. What would be the first steps to begin implementing this improvement? (Be specific.)

_____

_____

_____

_____

_____

_____

17. Other comments.

_____

_____

_____

_____

_____

_____

Additional Exercises:
To explore improvements in any or all of the other eight Quick-Tip areas from **Measuring and Analyzing Your Performance**, simply repeat this procedure using additional paper.

Notes

Water Cooler Wisdom

50 Quick Tips For Workplace Success!

Quick Tip Index

If you would like to...

★ Order additional copies of *Water Cooler Wisdom*...

★ Contact the author...

★ Express your opinion...

★ Tell us your favorite Quick-Tip...

★ Share your *Water Cooler Wisdom* success story...

★ Ask a question...

★ Tell us how you use *Water Cooler Wisdom* at work...

★ Learn how others use *Water Cooler Wisdom* to the fullest...

★ Find out more about our affiliate program...

★ Inquire about customer service training programs that work...

Visit us at
www.WaterCoolerWisdom.biz

Call: 1-800-974-5337
Fax: 1-802-985-5656

"A remarkably powerful yet simple book, written for everyone. It teaches with practical wisdom how to take control of your business life."

Dennis McDonough, President
Attitude & Response Management Systems

"Right on the money. Helps both managers and workers communicate about critical workplace and organizational needs and opportunities."

Thomas L. Davis, Director,
H.R./Productivity/Quality
Smugglers' Notch Resort

"The Quick-Tips in *Water Cooler Wisdom* are providing our workers with a better understanding of overall business and how our company runs. They like this book so they use it over and over. We are seeing positive performance improvements. Our eighty-one copies are a great employee development investment."

Doug Gobin, Principal
V-Tron Electronics

"Notable for its ideas, the fresh insights it offers, and a style that is marked by directness and clarity.... Useful to anyone regardless of where they work.... A genuine contribution to helping all workers be more responsible and effective."

Willy Schild, Ph.D., President
Critical Resources Group

"...educates the workforce on their role within the company and provides them with a necessary mini business education."

Nancy Binner, H.R. Manager
Acrotech Corp.

"When the boss gave us this book, it was weird – I never thought he would do something like that. It showed that he wants to help us... to put money into the people working for him, in turn to get better quality and expand in his business."

Doug Kendall
HVAC Control Technician

"...has obvious benefits for workers, clients, suppliers, and all other business associates."

John Coburn
Allstate Insurance Company

"...a wonderful resource for managers who want to promote responsibility in their employees."

Linda North, District Manager
Department of Health

"I actually felt honored when my boss handed me a copy. I looked up things that weren't working well for me... and the answers were right there – answers to the things that puzzled me."

Boris Thomas, Production Manager
Birnn Chocolates of Vermont

People like using the Quick-Tips in *Water Cooler Wisdom* because...

★ It covers such a wide range of concepts, all very important to workplace survival
★ It is written in plain English – so it can be easily understood at any level
★ It explains why "good business" is so important
★ It is concise, to the point, easy to read
★ It applies to all levels of employees
★ It can be used one topic at a time or in sections
★ It has brief, clear explanations in each paragraph
★ The concepts are meaningful for all phases of business, from the production floor to the management offices
★ It can be used as a basis of all training programs
★ It is a regular reminder – a reference tool to be used daily
★ It is a tremendous contribution to the workplace
★ It does a thorough job of conveying the general principles that form the basis for any successful organization
★ Its ideas are timely and relevant to today's workplace
★ It keeps people focused on the basics
★ It's like a way to "print money" – productivity increases

Simply stated – this book makes sense!